TO DRINK BOILED SNOW

CAROLINE

KNOX

WAVE BOOKS

TO DRINK BOILED

SNOW

SEATTLE & NEW YORK

PUBLISHED BY WAVE BOOKS

WWW.WAVEPOETRY.COM

COPYRIGHT © 2015 BY CAROLINE KNOX

WAVE BOOKS TITLES ARE DISTRIBUTED TO THE TRADE BY

CONSORTIUM BOOK SALES AND DISTRIBUTION

PHONE: 800-283-3572 / SAN 631-760X

LIBRARY OF CONGRESS CATALOGING-IN-PUBLICATION DATA

KNOX, CAROLINE.

[POEMS. SELECTIONS]

TO DRINK BOILED SNOW / CAROLINE KNOX. — FIRST EDITION.

PAGES ; CM

ISBN 978-1-940696-11-9

I. TITLE.

PS3561.N686A6 2015

811'.54—DC23

2014042284

DESIGNED AND COMPOSED BY QUEMADURA

PRINTED IN THE UNITED STATES OF AMERICA

9   8   7   6   5   4   3   2   1

FIRST EDITION

WAVE BOOKS 050

TO DRINK BOILED SNOW — 1

THE WORLD — 2

ALL GOOD — 4

WHEN I WAS ABOUT YOUR AGE, — 5

LOVE POEM — 8

PLAIN POEM — 9

SONG — 10

MOZART — 11

SLALOM — 13

DAVE THE POTTER MADE ME — 16

ISLANDS AND BRIDGES — 17

POEM BEGINNING WITH A LINE BY MILTON — 19

AN ONION — 20

THE ADVENTURE OF THE DANCING MEN — 21

THEY HAD HAD IT IN MIND — 22

PLATE 4 — 24

THE ERASERS — 25

POEM — 28

DIFFICULT EVENING — 29

WE SANG "FIRE! FIRE! MY HEART" — 30

ERA SURE — 31

BOUSTROPHEDON — 32

POEM FOR OTHER POEMS — 33

THAT ESCALATOR — 34

MAKE YOUR LAZINESS BE REAL REST — 35

MORGAN LE FAY — 36

OBJECTS — 37

ADDED CONCERN WITH EXTERNAL NATURE — 43

TITLE NOT GIVEN — 45

WHY WOULD THE MINOANS — 46

NOTES — 49

ACKNOWLEDGMENTS — 51

TO DRINK BOILED SNOW

TO DRINK BOILED SNOW

To drink boiled snow is good science.
It may affect the water table
to manufacture boiled snow on the rocks
218° Fahrenheit for however many minutes.

To skate on black ice is hard science
looking down through it to a broken and frozen rowboat
six feet under in Davy Jones's locker
in black tie in the middle of the night,

walking on thin ice, to skate on the
leading edge of thin ice, as abraded maple
leaves' patterns trip you up. To drink
unboiled sap as the deer do, clandestinely

out of sap buckets, starting on Birthington's Washday;
to discover in frozen sap
a distinctive new gelato! Flavor
of the month for March! To write

most of a poem out of
infinitive clauses, to discover
in brackish tidepools much too early
harbor seals in camouflage on the rocks,

and to marvel at these seals' poise and grace
as they blunder diffidently into and below the ocean.

THE WORLD

You think the world re-
volves around you, well it
revolves around Copernicus
and around Ortelius of whom
you've never even heard, you
idiot. Who has? You act
like you're inside the Boston
Mapparium, the spherical
stained-glass window
that's meant to show you
where continents are.
Now space is elastic
(and so is matter, but
space a lot more so).
We know it's elastic because of
Ortelius, who saw that long ago
the continents imperceptibly
had broken off from one another.
The Mapparium makes you feel
you're the core of the earth,
churning liquid fire. You're not,
though—no one is, and
it's very irritating to be so
misled, mistaught. Item: Marco
Polo is a swimming pool
game. The It person yells
Marco with eyes shut and
everyone else yells Polo

2

and tries not to get tagged.
Or it's—Item—a restaurant
game, you go into a café and
yell Marco and if it's the right
restaurant someone yells
Polo and you win concert
tickets. Remember that smart
video called *Voices and Visions*
gathering poems and critics in
1988? Mark Strand said there
and then: "Stevens's disclosures
are not of the primary sort,"
a comforting, useful sentence
for stymied readers that
might be applied to the case
of the planet's core and surface.
It's probably all for the best
that continents were broken off
to where they be right now. If
it's the wrong restaurant, you'd
feel like a jerk. You don't have gills
like fish to swim between and among
the continents in international waters.

ALL GOOD

What would we do without
sidereal time? ("He did not know
how far away / everything was
from each other.") What would we?
All good, Allsorts
(Hundreds and Thousands)!
What was it called, not
binomial nomenclature
("He had to crawl down
three flights of sleep
to stare at breakfast worry")
in Algebra II when there were
two equations in two unknowns
("If you lived here, you'd be home now")
and you couldn't solve that,
and after a browbeating
but oh yes you could, all good
—not nomenclature, binomial
theorem? What is it with
words like *sidereal*?
Side + real?
which means "of stars" and "of stones"
at the same time; how could it?
There is no word like *sidereal*.
We should take it all in good part.
There is no word like *sidereal*.

my great-aunt, who was the
librarian of Vassar College,
gave me an old navy-blue book,
The Oxford Book of English Verse.
It was from 1942. Back then,
it was amazing that a girl could
have a major librarian job like
that, but she did. So I read and read it,
and some of the book was in
weird-looking English. About
a third of the way through there is a
poem called "The Rime of the Ancient
Mariner," by Samuel Taylor Coleridge.
I think you'd like it a lot because
you're an experienced cruising sailor,
and you have a great science sense,
and you like challenges. It's about
a trip to the South Pole, it's told
by one of the sailors, to a man he meets;
it's a ghost story and a nature story.
It's full of surprises, like this one:
"The Sun came up upon the left, /
Out of the sea came he!" Really?
The sun came out of the sea?
Well, no. But it's a
great way to talk about the
power and speed of the sun.

Anyway, there was an
artist in France, Gustave Doré,
who loved the "Rime," too, and
he made pictures, engravings,
to show what he thought
the voyage was like. Please
google Doré and see what
you think.

        Coleridge and Doré
both loved to be scared, and
they loved joy, too. They
loved to make fear and joy
together in art. Coleridge
would go on walking
tours with his friends
by lakes and mountains.
Another poem in the book,
much shorter, is "Kubla Khan."
Kubla was king
in China. He built
a palace called
"a stately pleas-
ure dome," which meant
a real palace and
a palace of poetry
both at the same time. Coleridge
loved to do several
things at once.
And anyway,
this book, *The Oxford*

Book of English
Verse, used to be mine,
and now it's
yours, your name
is in it for good.

LOVE POEM

A man brings a
woman a chop from
China, in his lap on
the plane: it is a
basalt seal and is
topped by a bird,
red-dotted eyes.

She says oh, oh, I
love this grayish bird
his dotted eyes, the
striated feathers so
unlike the shiny base.

Oh, the chop prints
two ideograms:
I am Lark Crowe
You're Jay Wren
I guess we're a rebus.

PLAIN POEM

You had your eye on the (peeling) brackets
of the residential mansard on our way out of town; my attention
was drawn to its egg-and-dart railing cusp
in which there was no waste: if not egg,
then dart, if not dart, then egg. You
were riveted by a rooftop party we could almost touch,
and, in the underpasses, dripping soffits absorbed us.
A flange of ivy absorbed us. I think this was
vicarious Stamford, pale buildings oblique to the train.

SONG

Down come the yellow tickets
The mower makes dust of the leaves
Tears spring to the eyes
brushed away by snows

La la la la snows
La la la la eyes

I gave my love a copy
of *The Education of Henry Adams*
He gave me a subscription
to *The Journal of Fonzarelli Studies*
We went beside the river
in the snow sleet snow

La la la la *Adams*
La la la la *Studies*

There is a tree in the park
they call the hackmatack
Its other name is tamarack
Its other other name is larch
Calling all birds, it's time, birds
time to go wheeling south

La la la la tickets
La la la la south
La la la la yellow
La la la la river

MOZART

Can you imagine
what is true, that
smack in the middle
of making *The Magic
Flute* he interrupted
himself to make
"Ave verum corpus,"
world's most truth-telling
motet (Who made its
text? Maybe a pope),
then got himself on
track, back to *TMF*
(all the while dealing
with money-worry and
sickness of wife). When
you hear the *esto nobis*
cadence in "AVC," you
scale the spine of the
European Enlightenment;
when you hear the
idiotic chorus "Three
Faithful Youths" in
The Magic Flute—

> "Three faithful youths we now will lend you
> Upon your journey they'll attend you
> Though young in years these youths so fair
> Heed the words of wisdom rare!"

—you're dealing with
Bertie Wooster's
three best friends.
Because he was Mozart,
not a problem.

SLALOM

In *The Mitten*,
by Tresselt and
Yaroslava,
and also in
Red Fox and his
Canoe, by Na-
thaniel Benchley
—in both these books—
large numbers of
beasts attempt to
(respectively)
hide in a huge
mitten, and board
a boat. It's an
old story, and
as with Alex
Katz's paintings,
limited in-
formation is
disclosed. Folktales
aren't *by* any-
one, anyway.
Sarah and Bill
and Grace and Moll-
y and Emma
went down the San
Juan River in
kayaks. There were

seven kayaks
full of cousins
with them. When they
got into the
remote parts, where
there were pueblos
(or what was left
over from them),
kayakers from
earlier had
landed, searched the
caves and laid out
pottery shards
in even rows,
arrowheads and
maybe mortars
and pestles? Or
just interest-
ing stones. No one
for miles and miles
down the winding
San Juan River
in Arizona
snaking in a
slalom length of
dimeter for
Demeter, who
really deserves
fourteeners in
her odes, consid-
ering her mag-

nanimity,
or uppercase
majesty, as
DEMETER, which
is an acro-
nym for Detec-
tion of Elec-
tro-Magnetic
Emission Trans-
mitted from Earth-
quake Regions.
It comes from France.

DAVE THE POTTER MADE ME

I am a made thing, a jar incised with cursive writing;
the poem is in my shoulders.
Glaze oozes down into the lettering and is fired there,

and Dave closes the complete rhyme.
His new adage is the poem.

Dave writes with a wet knife
while my leather-hard sides
are still wet. 1832, he writes
    Dave belongs to Mr. Miles
    Where the oven bakes and the pot biles

—My sides have a green glaze
like tears caught and fired:
    I wonder where is all my friends and relations
    Friendship to all in every nation

—over and under dripped,
ochre and umber,
along the rolled rim down
for each master: Drake, Gibbs, Miles, Landrum.

ISLANDS AND BRIDGES

You are in Woods Hole now and you go to
the Vineyard and you are on the Vineyard. You
go next to Nantucket and you are on Nantucket.
You go to Ceylon and to Cuba. Are you on them?
You go to Japan, which is islands, and you are in
Japan. But when you
cross from Manhattan on the Brooklyn Bridge
into Brooklyn, you're on Long Island
and in Brooklyn too at the same time.
The Tappan Zee Bridge is said to be
crumbling, can't make up its
mind—straight shot or arc—
no, both. It's my favorite bridge
and so is the causeway on
Lake Pontchartrain. A toll bridge
spans the Sakonnet River from
Tiverton, RI, to Newport: the toll makes it too
expensive for hard-pressed commuters
to take the bridge to work, how should
they then live. Newport is on
Aquidneck Island. No bridges
take you to Haiti or Barbados
now, or Rhodes or Skiathos.
The Széchenyi chain-bridge is
in Budapest, which is

a dactyl, as is *anapest*.
This bridge connects
Pest with Buda.
This poem connects
islands with bridges.

POEM BEGINNING WITH A LINE BY MILTON

It was the winter wild
when we found *ilex verticillata*,
a deciduous holly, growing
spontaneously in the
sophisticated taupe landscape.
Of its yellow-scarlet berries, Asa Gray
wrote: "nutlets smooth and even."
The holly's leaves were down, dead,
and mashed by rain. Why
didn't birds go after those berries,
in this poem which
ends with a line by
Creeley: the story is true.

PLATE 4

Even if you slowly scrutinize Audubon's
Plate 4 (1827), it's hard to see
the rattler preparing insidiously to appropriate
the eggs of Northern Mockingbirds and
presently the mockingbirds themselves.
A trumpet vine obscures the threat.

Today for food, shelter, light, wind,
water, heat, this same bird panics,
and ranges far north for food, shelter,
light, wind, water, heat; food,
shelter, light, wind, water, heat.

THE ERASERS

PENCIL ERASER

LARGE OBLONG RUBBER ERASER

BLACKBOARD ERASER

WHITEBOARD ERASER

SCRUBBING BRUSH

BUCKET

SWIFFER

WITE-OUT

(Scene: Kansas.)

LARGE OBLONG RUBBER ERASER:
    This blank-verse poem takes the form of a play
    but isn't one; the characters have connections
    with erasure; they have jobs to do
    and words to say. At issue here is what
    we need to have erased, and who should do it.

WHITEBOARD ERASER:
    My method is Magnetic Dry-Erase.

SCRUBBING BRUSH (to Bucket):
    Bucket, doesn't this project seem to you
    like when Robert Rauschenberg proposed
    to erase a drawing of something by Willem de Kooning?

BUCKET:
    It is in fact a little bit like that.

SCRUBBING BRUSH:
    And then de Kooning said it was okay.

BLACKBOARD ERASER:

    The type in which the names of our roles are set
    is just the one employed by Samuel French
    to indicate the person speaking next
    on every page of every drama text.
    The font is called SMALL CAPS. And it remains
    to place an alexandrine as this stanza's plinth.

PENCIL ERASER:

    Come off it, this is meant to be blank verse.
    What needs to be erased, and why do you
    believe that we're the ones to do the job?
    And I don't like the chalk dust everywhere.

(Enter ALLEGORY.*)*

BLACKBOARD ERASER:

    Now who comes here?

ALLEGORY:

    My name is Allegory.

WHITEBOARD ERASER:

    This name does not appear upon the list
    of Dramatis Personae. Who are you?

ALLEGORY:

    An emanation from the chrism of
    the indeterminate, I move through time
    and space, through syncope and vacuity.
    I don't see why I should be on that list:

I figure as an allegory only,
and can possess no character as such.
I stand among the company of erasers,
but you probably couldn't erase me if you tried!

(*Enter* IRONY.)

IRONY:

Now, Allegory, this is where your toes
turn in, for Kenneth Koch has written
in what is much admired as his best work,
"Some General Instructions," that "the days
of / Allegory are over," and "The Days
of Irony are here."

ALLEGORY:

How are you, Irony?
And since you bring it up, you know you are
a prime example of an allegory,
since you personify an abstract concept!

BUCKET:

Wouldn't we like to have some lemonade?
Swiffer, have a glass.

SWIFFER:

Oh, thank you, Bucket.

(*Enter* WITE-OUT, *who paints
all over* OMNES. *Curtain.*)

POEM

Of milk, these persons make the butter until have
what are cheeses when they're at home;
of cheese, hors d'oeuvres of sandwich are manufactured
sandwich islands. The workforce custom subsume
draft cereal. Forasmuch as we
are not birdlike, we pig out, crikey,
put away comestibles big-time.
Now of festal song where I come from
inaccessible, we call it the Sangfroid,
venue most regal, velvet porte cocheres,
SATB separate sections, coherence, memorize
text, listen to every, glower at conductor,
impact procedure not yawning,
not singing with likewise mouths
full of notes, everybody in mode mode.

DIFFICULT EVENING

Their job is to write the place cards, so at the head of the table
they are putting Gilbert Osmond, and honorably on his right
they seat Margot Macomber. Next to Margot, Montresor
is to sit beside Zenobia Frome; then,
John Claggart, master-at-arms of the *Bellipotent*.
At G.O.'s left, Dr. Tamkin,
and on *his* left, Pap Finn.
Thus there are nine guests:
at the foot of the table they put Madame Merle, so she and G.O.
will have to look directly at one another the whole time, and won't she have fun
talking to her neighbor on the right, Young Goodman Brown.

which is difficult,
and meant it, which is easy
Maybe Thomas Morley wrote
the text as well as notes
to this madrigal: "Oh! I burn me"
Did he mean it? He meant it
in unsingable diphthongs:
Fire, Fire, I, Ay, Cry nigh
and easy-to-make sloppy,
hard-to-make-crisp
entrances—difficult, to make
his trouble our trouble,
his short vowels our short vowels:
help, sit, none comes, burn
quench and drench. But oh!
it's the broken dishwasher
that slops and drenches
the kitchen floor and then I
burn me on the difficult stove, I mean it
Aloe vera, easy botanical
soothing, come and quench
Help, I sit and cry me sorely
in triphthongs like an a cappella *Aiieee*!

ERA SURE

Bottles of the white stuff   matte
          Quid ape, otherwise
"A Polar Bear Eating Marshmallows in a Snowstorm"
Everywhere many
bottles of white matte Liquid Paper
                      quid   ape
                      qui   a
                        id   ap
otherwise a droodle

Whiteout whiteout!
  hit   out!
                     (id   ap)

   it   ut
   hi   o

BOUSTROPHEDON

Your oxen may be quite large, and to push GEE
them around in one direction may not be easy; HAW
this is a good reason to train them when they are GEE
young. Then they tend to be more submissive. HAW
People took a huge picnic down to the meadows GEE
and teamsters were sleeping, stuffed with lunch. HAW
Don't forget to use your ox's name—then he will GEE
know you are talking to him alone of the team. HAW
Oxen dreamed of cowslips in the shade, muzzles GEE
stained from grazing. Who knows what the cuds HAW
led them to think in those precincts. Congratulate GEE
your ox for turning so nicely. A good deal of an HAW
ox's learning will take place after he starts work. GEE
Weary trainers urged the team homeward from the HAW
completion of deep furrows in a parallelogram. WHOA

POEM FOR OTHER POEMS

A poem for "She Leaves to Sleep," by Rachel Hinton: parallel

structure (times, Leaving early, Thick-crusted . . . pizza, Errands, Coffee).

Then the Marianne Moore arrangement—not coming back to a premise! A poem

for Roberto Bolaño's "Labyrinth," where wrong information is planted, even the wrong

plant information (just look at the photograph). And who's to say what clothing is of "good quality"

or who is "the handsomest." This is a poem for "Happy Fainting," by Katia

Kapovich, "armed with a red marker," doing "magazine stuff"; after all,

write wherever you can "find a flat surface," said

John Cheever. For Margaret Fuller,

who in 1840 wrote that Chicago was "a giant valve."

This poem is for profound "Bermudas,"

by Marvell; it's for Michael Dennis Browne's

"Peter"—"Not knows why. But does. / Not knows why. But is"; and for

Julio Cortázar, in *Cronopios and Famas*: "[T]he famas are good [at heart] and the esperanzas are blockheads."

THAT ESCALATOR

That escalator at O'Hare where you go flat along the floor
    forward without moving your feet from the granular surface
without moving your suitcase or satchel, instead of inching
    jerkily upward at Union Station–New Haven say
with two railings to hold on to as you block people
    gracefully trying to get where they're going—
that escalator, which doesn't escalate, makes you feel like
    a confused duck, you might tip over. Clueless feet
in elevator shoes or stilettos (left and right, one for each foot)
    support the crocodile of passive humanity, and are now off
to board and take flight for ultimately Nome or New Bedford
    in toes, taps, mukluks; in mary janes, jellies,
wellies, trainers, brogues—take flight for where? My husband
    occasionally taught a class at O'Hare, his students flew in
from fieldwork in Wauregan or Pierre to exchange thoughts,
    and then flew out again. But you might not, you might stay
right on the belt, as part of an installation.
    You can make the ending first and let that tell you
what came before, in traction there where we "stood":
    frozen in a frieze that moved us along often
and constantly, among Hoosiers, high-profile Assyrians.

MAKE YOUR LAZINESS BE REAL REST

Make your laziness be real rest; why should you throw out useful sloth—
it's there because you need it; you should think about practical emptiness.
About what? Make your loafing real rest, make a deliberate ruin for it.
Make a ruin and be its anchorite in empty time; make a run for it.
Make a rune for your laziness, and now with your ears you
hear the breath of grass and wind, of stones turned to water
in lazy time. Heed the numinosity of a laziness rune; it's imperative to
see a rune with your eyes shut, holding the shaded image
in a historical light! Fallow earth is lazy and productive when we
touch it, knowing its rest in time, and as we remember it from youth.
The sun makes laziness volatile. Rays lift the air everywhere somehow,
harsh- and/or sweet-smelling, and we know it, but while lolling
about we don't register clearly, and isn't that okay. Emptier things:
a mind a blank, a mind a haze, a mind a black polished screen, turning
from meaning. Your laziness can be real rest, make it craftsmanlike, a devotion.

MORGAN LE FAY

Ay, glean from
agony, Mr. Leaf.
Manage rolfy
Yale FM groan.
Ogle any farm.
Yale FM groan
gone. Flay ram!
Mangle foray!
Foamy angler,
rage of manly
moray flange!
Lo, mange fray:
my flea organ!
Many a golfer
lame or fangy.
Ay, angel form!

OBJECTS

"I only owe the university three hundred
dollars, and if I can't get it I
can't graduate with the class."
Karen said this to Sarah, and
went out to read bulletin boards.
POETRY READING CONTEST
THREE HUNDRED DOLLARS
FIRST PRIZE. Karen registered
and got up on the stage and read
"Sunday Morning," won, and graduated.
"You never forget a beautiful
thing that you have made," said Chef
Bugnard of the Cordon Bleu
to Julia Child, "even after you
eat it, it stays with you—*always*."

* * *

If you visit the homestead
of Frederick Law Olmsted
in Brookline, Massachusetts,
a docent may say something
like this to you: "Look
around at the flowers."
There isn't one flower there,
but every shade of green
leaf and needle and spear.
Olmsted didn't want flowers.

Introducing her poem "Kyoto"
at Sackler Museum in maybe
2003, Jorie Graham
said, "Our relationship with
the environment is
complicated, but it's
not difficult." On the same
occasion, she went on to say,
of an ikebana poem, "The
autobiographical parts are true."

* * *

These are the words
of Robert Darvin,
a Haitian refugee
evicted from a
tent camp, of his
new and flimsy
home: "It is made
of cheap cement.
If you think too
much about it
you lose your mind."
Samuel Sewall wrote,
"Sabbath . . . This day
so cold that the
Sacramental Bread
is frozen pretty hard,
and rattles sadly
as broken into the Plates."

* * *

A composer's mom said
to him, "How do you
know what notes to
write on the staff?"
"Mom," he said, "I
hear them in my head."
Peter Williams, in his
magisterial biography
of Bach, opined that
the Coffee Cantata and
the Peasant Cantata
are as close as Bach
got to writing opera.

* * *

This is a translation of the swimming match
description in *Beowulf*, where Unferth
is doing his damnedest to discredit the hero:
"Are you the same Beowulf who held with Breca
a notorious swimming race on the open sea?
Impelled by pride and boasting, you risked your lives
on the deep. Nor could anyone, friend or foe, dissuade you
from this foolhardy swimming scheme. So there you were:
you struck out into the current as if embracing
the sea-streams, which boiled around you, with your arms.
Seven nights you toiled in the water's power.
Then Breca's skill and endurance overmatched you
and the sea in the morning bore him to the shore

of the Heatho-Reams, and then to his own home,
his people, castle, treasure. The son of Beanstan
carried out the word of his boast to you in deed;
thus I expect it will go much the same
with you again, despite your fame in battle,
if you dare to watch through the night with Grendel here."

* * *

"The research highlighted
that one critical component
to building the capacity
of strategic execution is
the establishment of a
value attitude." This
sentence has so much
wrong with it that you
hardly know where to
start. At least it doesn't
have topic drift, or does it.

* * *

A salad: chopped
cucumbers, chopped
romaine, blueberries,
fresh mint, feta
cheese; for dressing: oil
and vinegar, and a
little honey. In a
bowl, stainless steel

rimmed with beading,
making clunks of noise
with serving tools, on
a cloth, a blue cotton,
on a table, maybe
maple, maybe
refinished by Alan
Marbury, an
accomplished
woodworker.

* * *

Flora Thompson wrote, "The
hamlet laughed at
the village as 'stuck up';
while the village looked
down on 'that gipsy lot'
at the hamlet." And Angela
Thirkell wrote of
a child's thoughts:
"No one quite under-
stood what [the boy]
meant and by the time
he had spoken, what he
said appeared to
him to be meaningless.
We have all had that
experience." And
finally—clear-eyed
and incisive—Laurie

Capps wrote, "We are
all / issued white
coats; we are
forever / taking
samples of the world."

Above, the big stroppy pale green leaves
of ill-fated *Acer pseudoplatanus*
trees standing up dead,
a long time seasoning themselves
until felled and cut, split
and stacked up ready to burn:
this maple doesn't live long, ten
or fifteen years tops; there is
even a *purpurascens* variety
if you can stand it; Bailey says so.
A. pseudoplatanus looks like a
cheesy version of the
elegant tulip tree,
Liriodendron tulipifera:
my neighbor and I walked and walked,
stared at a tulip tree fifty feet over us—
there's a tree worth looking at, full
bloom, yellow cups, dark crisp leaves,
tulips as offered civilly on plates,
satisfying tree truly worth looking at.
We were discussing the
protozoa—amoebas, paramecia,
hydras, more, all motile, nucleate.
Of all the one-celled creatures,
I said that I liked hydras best;
my neighbor liked the amoeba,
which puts out pseudopods when
needed, much more genuine

than the *pseudoplatanus*
masquerading as a plane tree. And
practical! We agreed that
protozoa are cute; we agreed that
it would be nice to be one-celled,
as you would only have one job
and you would know what it
was, and you would do it all
the time, no stress! Well, maybe.
What if you were an invertebrate?
Microbeworld.com says,
"They teem in the deep sea."
So she went home and I went
home hungry as John McPhee's bear
who ate a blueberry bush;
I ate granola and Greek yoghurt.
Next day my neighbor on the
other side showed up and we
looked at some weeds and had no
idea what they were.
"Let's make up a name," he said,
"*Areopagitica canadensis*."
But *Areopagitica* is no joke:
"We boast our light," John Milton
wrote, "but if we look not
wisely on the Sun itself,
it smites us into darkness."

TITLE NOT GIVEN

Information delayed. Information withheld.
Saturation with info, useless and helpful blended. Plot
not "completed." Size and significance of events
unemphatic: *far* too much attention paid to
tiny subjects. Option on funny noises.
Order of info homogeneous. Litotes, a Greek god,
Litotes of Lacedaemonia. Why isn't this boring?
Do I need this info? It changes all the time,
doesn't repeat itself, it only almost does.
What is a "conditional honorific"?
Randomness and inductive method, both at once.
"So what?" is a valuable question to ask. Frame story,
like *Taming of the Shrew*, but W.S. didn't
finish the frame! A is really a pretext for B. B is what counts.

WHY WOULD THE MINOANS

Why would the Minoans fire the
clay tablets that they recorded their
everyday transactions on? They
wouldn't and didn't, so when the

rotted thatched roof of the rented
house of Arthur Evans fell in during a
prodigious downpour, all the unfired
gray clay tablets unreadable as yet and ever

"cut out by me in one piece with their
earthly matrix," wrote the discoverer,
"had already been reduced to a pulpy mass."
To even get started, Evans had to

buy some of Knossos. To deal with
language barriers, he spoke Latin
with priests. Klutzy, Evans said the only
sport he was good at was

jumping to conclusions,
although right out of Oxford, he and
his brother Lewis hiked and hiked in the Balkans
"armed with Bologna sandwiches and Turkish delight."

Older than Oxford by a long chalk,
Bologna is the first continuous
university: 1088 CE. How
terrific that Bologna sandwiches fed

and feed millions of students! Did
the eponymous Earl of Sandwich go
to Oxford? Trinity Cambridge.
Bologna is home to Luigi

Galvani, who discovered
galvanism. Lokum is
the real name for Turkish delight.
No confection is more beautiful.

NOTES

"Poem Beginning with a Line by Milton": John Milton, "Ode on the Morning of Christ's Nativity," *Paradise Regained, the Minor Poems, and Samson Agonistes* (Odyssey Press, 1927), 152; Asa Gray, *Gray's New Manual of Botany* (American Book Co., 1908), 555; Robert Creeley, "Bresson's Movies," *Postmodern American Poetry, A Norton Anthology*, Second Edition, ed. Paul Hoover (Norton, 2013), 135.

"An Onion": Howard Norman, *I Hate to Leave This Beautiful Place* (Houghton Mifflin, 2013), 2.

"Boustrophedon": Material on ox training is taken from www.iscowp.org/ox-power-handbook-lesson-4.html.

"Poem for Other Poems": Rachel Hinton, "She Leaves to Sleep," *Denver Quarterly* 46/4, 52; Roberto Bolaño, "Labyrinth," *New Yorker*, January 23, 2012, 67 (trans. Chris Andrews); Katia Kapovich, "Happy Fainting," *Cossacks and Bandits* (Salt, 2008), 61; Blake Bailey, *Cheever: A Life* (Knopf, 2009), 258; John Matteson, *The Lives of Margaret Fuller* (Norton, 2012), 224; Michael Dennis Browne, "Peter," *New Yorker*, April 9, 1966, 91; Julio Cortázar, *Cronopios and Famas* (Pantheon, 1969), 134 (trans. Paul Blackburn).

"Objects": Julia Child, *My Life in France* (Anchor, 2007), 65; Robert Darvin, Quotation of the Day, *New York Times*, April 24, 2011, A3; Samuel Sewall, *Diary*, entry for January 24, 1686; Peter Williams, *J. S. Bach: A Life in Music* (Cambridge University Press, 2007), 222, 292–5; Flora Thompson, *Lark Rise to Candleford* (Godine, 2009), 36; Angela Thirkell, *Love at All Ages* (Knopf, 1959), 203; Laurie Capps, "Practice Test," *Denver Quarterly* 45/3, 2011, 10.

"Why would the Minoans": Arthur J. Evans, *Scripta Minoa* (Clarendon, 1909), 42, 61; Margalit Fox, *The Riddle of the Labyrinth* (Ecco, 2013), 67–68; Sylvia L. Horwitz, *The Find of a Lifetime* (Sterling, 2001), 26, 32, 81, 88.

ACKNOWLEDGMENTS

Grateful acknowledgment is made to the magazines in which poems from *To Drink Boiled Snow* first appeared: "To Drink Boiled Snow" and "The world"—expressmilwaukee.com; "All Good"—*Superstition Review*; "When I was about your age"—*Tin House*; "Love Poem" and "Poem"—*Map Literary*; "Plain Poem" and "Make your laziness be real rest"—*Denver Quarterly*; "Song," "The Adventure of the Dancing Men," "Plate 4," and "That escalator"—thecommononline.org; "Mozart"—poets.org; "Slalom"—*Sixth Finch*; "An Onion," "Dave the Potter Made Me," "We Sang 'Fire! Fire! My Heart,'" "Erasure," and "Boustrophedon"—*New American Writing*; "Islands and Bridges" and "Added Concern with External Nature"—*Hanging Loose*; "Poem Beginning with a Line by Milton" and "Title Not Given"—*Divine Magnet*; "They had had it in mind"—*The Common*; "The Erasers"—*Yew Journal*; "Difficult Evening"—*A Public Space*; "Poem for Other Poems"—*Coconut*; "Morgan le Fay"—*Fou*; "Objects"—*Superstition Review* (except for translation of *Beowulf* VIII: 506–528, *Washington Square*); "Why Would the Minoans"—*The Baffler*.

Fourteen poems were published in an artist's book/chapbook in the Fall 2013 series edited by Jason Dodge of Fivehundred Places (fivehundredplaces.com).

Many, many thanks to Matthew Zapruder, Joshua Beckman, and Jeff Clark for great wisdom.